101 FACTS ABOUT

GUINEA PIGS

Published by Ringpress Books Limited,
PO Box 8, Lydney, Gloucestershire,
GL15 4YN, United Kingdom.

Design: Sara Howell

First Published 2001
© 2001 RINGPRESS BOOKS LIMITED

ISBN 1 86054 138 0

Printed in Hong Kong through Printworks Int. Ltd.

0 9 8 7 6 5 4 3 2 1

101 FACTS ABOUT

GUINEA PIGS

Julia Barnes

Ringpress Books

2 The guinea pig's home is Peru in South America. They used to live in large family groups, known as colonies, in the Andes mountains.

3 The wild guinea pigs found their homes in little gaps among the rocks or in burrows that had been given up by other small animals. They grazed on grass and wild plants.

1 Guinea pigs are one of the most popular pets to keep. They are gentle, they like people, and they hardly ever bite or scratch.

4 Guinea pigs were highly valued by the **Incas** who lived in Peru – but not as pets. They were sacrificed and eaten on special occasions.

5 Today there are no guinea pigs left in the wild, but they are kept as pets in many countries.

6 Nobody knows how the guinea pig got its name. They are not related to pigs, but perhaps when you see a smooth-haired guinea pig trot, it may remind you of a pig!

7 Guinea Pigs are also known as **cavies**; breeders and other experts prefer to use that name.

8 Animals are divided into groups which share the same basic habits. Guinea pigs belong to the **rodent** group, which includes mice, rats, hamsters, chinchillas, and porcupines.

9 These animals may seem very different, but all rodents are gnawing animals, and have teeth that grow all the time.

10 Guinea pigs are most closely related to coypus porcupines and chinchillas, which come from South and Central America and the Caribbean Islands.

11 Guinea pigs usually live for around six years, but they can survive much longer than that.

12 The oldest recorded pet guinea pig was Snowball, from Nottinghamshire, England, who died in February 1979 at the grand old age of 14 years and 10 months.

13 An adult female is called a **sow**, and an adult male is called a **boar**.

14 A sow weighs around 30 oz (850 g); a boar weighs around 35 oz (992 g).

15 Pet guinea pigs like to live in small groups. It is best to keep two or three sows. Adult boars that are kept together may well fight.

16 Some people like to keep rabbits and guinea pigs together, but guinea pigs are very timid and can end up being bullied. A female of one of the smaller breeds of rabbit would make the best companion, but the two animals must be introduced at an early age.

17 You can buy a guinea pig from any good pet store, where experienced staff can advise you.

18 DON'T buy a sickly guinea pig just because you feel sorry for it. You could end up with a lot of heartache and expense trying to get it well.

19 DO choose a young guinea pig at around six weeks of age, so that it will be easy to tame with plenty of gentle handling.

20 A healthy guinea pig should be lively, curious and active. These are the checks you can make:

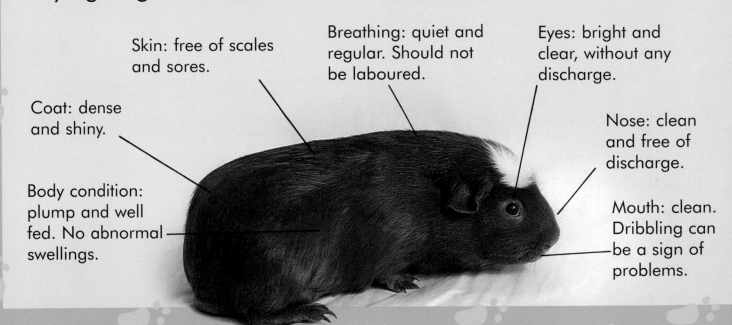

Skin: free of scales and sores.

Breathing: quiet and regular. Should not be laboured.

Eyes: bright and clear, without any discharge.

Coat: dense and shiny.

Nose: clean and free of discharge.

Body condition: plump and well fed. No abnormal swellings.

Mouth: clean. Dribbling can be a sign of problems.

21 Ask an expert to check whether the guinea pig is a boar or a sow before making your choice.

22 Guinea pigs come in three main varieties:

- **Smooth** (short-coated – often known as the English, American or Bolivian breeds).
- **Abyssinian** (a rougher coat arranged in circular shapes known as whorls and rosettes – right).
- **Long-haired** (this includes the long-coated Peruvian).

23 Most stores sell **crossbred** guinea pigs, which make ideal pets. If you want a **purebred** guinea pig (perhaps you want to get involved with showing), you will need to go to a specialist breeder.

24 There are some more unusual coat types that have resulted from special breeding programmes. These include **Rex** (a woolly coat that stands upright), and **Satin** (a short coat that is very shiny).

▲ A Satin Cream.

25 There is a wide range of guinea pig colours and markings. A guinea pig may be one colour **(self)**, or a combination of colours **(marked)**.

▲ A Silver-and-white Agouti Rex.

26 Guinea pig coat patterns include Agouti (two shades of colour on each hair), Himalayan (a light-coloured body with

◀ A spotted Dalmatian.

Siamese type markings), Dalmatian (a black head, a white body and black spots), Tortoiseshell (patterned with blocks of black and red), and Dutch (white with colour markings).

27 There are many other interesting varieties, such as the American Crested, a self-coloured guinea pig with a crest of contrasting colour.

28 The Silkie (or Sheltie) is another long-haired variety. Its long, soft coat grows backwards from the nose and over its back. It is shaped rather like a tear-drop.

29 All purebred show guinea pigs are judged by a Breed Standard, which describes the perfect size, shape, colour and coat type for that particular variety.

▲ A Dutch Red.

30 Smooth-haired guinea pigs are the best choice for a novice owner, as they are hardy, good-natured and do not need very much grooming.

31 Guinea pigs are especially difficult to treat, so you need to find a guinea pig-friendly vet in your area that is experienced in caring for small animals.

32 Guinea pigs are not as tough as rabbits. If they are housed outdoors, they should be brought into an outside shed during the winter.

33 Do not use a garage to house your guinea pigs – the fumes from a car could kill them.

34 Buy the biggest **hutch** you can afford. The minimum size should be 3ft wide, 2ft deep, and 18 inches high (91 cms x 61 cms x 45 cms).

35 The hutch should be on legs, at least nine inches (23 cms) from the ground to protect the guinea pigs from draughts.

36 The hutch must have secure fastenings to keep the guinea pigs from breaking out, and to prevent enemies, such as dogs or cats, from breaking in.

37 The wire-netting (mesh) on the front of the hutch must be narrow enough to stop mice and rats from getting in.

38 Hutches come in many different types of design. Here are the basic features a guinea pig requires to be comfortable in his home:

Private sleeping area.

Secure fastening.

Raised legs to stop the guinea pigs being affected by draughts.

Wire-netting to keep mice and rats away.

39 Some guinea pigs are kept in the house in specially-designed cages. The cage should be kept in a quiet room, such as a utility room.

40 Guinea pigs have very sensitive hearing, and can be upset by loud noises. It is best not to keep them in a room with a television or a radio.

41 If you keep your guinea pig in an indoor cage, you will need to provide an exercise run. This can be a shallow-sided tray, lined with wood shavings. It should measure around 12 ft^2 (3.66 m^2) for two or three guinea pigs.

42 Some owners allow their guinea pigs to run free in a small area of the house. This should be made completely safe, with no cables or other hazards. Remember, guinea pigs love to gnaw, so wooden furniture should be removed.

43 Make sure you watch your guinea pig closely when he is out of his cage, or he will be swift to find his own hiding places.

44 Guinea pigs can be house-trained to use a litter tray (rather like a cat). The trick is to keep the guinea pig in a small area where he can get at the litter tray, and he should start using it. Never be angry if he makes a mistake.

45 A guinea pig needs plenty of bedding in his home to keep him warm.

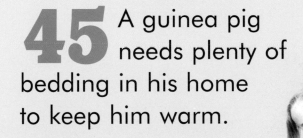

46 The best bedding is wood shavings with a top layer of hay. Do not use straw as the sharp ends could hurt your guinea pig.

47 Guinea pigs need fresh water at all times. The best way to provide this is with a water-bottle, attached to the side of the hutch or cage.

48 Guinea pigs like to throw their food around, so provide heavy, bowls that they cannot tip over. A hay-rack is also useful.

49 Unlike rodents such as hamsters, rats and mice, guinea pigs do not play with toys, but they do appreciate places to hide. Cut some holes in a cardboard box, and you can enjoy watching your guinea pigs scurrying in and out.

50 Provide some pipe tunnels in the run, perhaps leading to a secret supply of food, and your guinea pigs will love investigating.

51 In the summer, guineas pigs like being outside in a run where they can graze and exercise. Part of the run must be in the shade – and you must remember to attach a water-bottle.

52 Guinea pigs love to sunbathe – but they can overdo it. White animals are prone to sunburn, particularly on the ears. It is best to take your guinea pigs outside in the early morning or the late afternoon when the sun is not so hot.

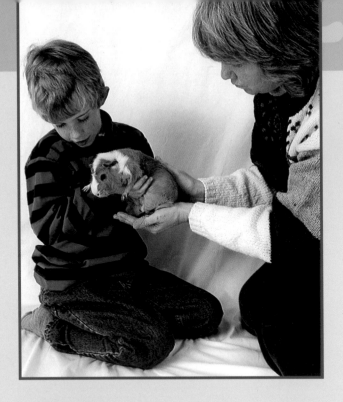

newcomer. Put lots of food in the outside run, and allow the guinea pigs to feed together. Make sure the new arrival has been accepted before putting the guinea pigs in their sleeping area.

53 Do not overwhelm the guinea pig with too much attention when you first bring him home. Give him a chance to settle and to explore his new surroundings.

54 If you already have guinea pigs at home, it is not difficult to introduce a

55 The correct way to hold a guinea pig is to grasp him around his shoulders, supporting his weight with your other hand under his rear end.

56 A complete diet is provided by pet stores in flaked or pellet form, and guinea pigs do well on it.

57 Hay should be given freely at all times. Guinea pigs prefer the soft meadow hay rather than the coarser type.

58 Guinea pigs and humans share something in common – we cannot make Vitamin C in our own bodies. This vitamin is very important – without it we could get a condition called scurvy, which is a killer.

59 So, we must get our Vitamin C by eating fresh fruit and vegetables, which guinea pigs need to eat, too.

62 Guinea pigs love lettuce, but it can cause health problems if it is fed in large amounts. This also applies to cabbage – it is best to feed the outer leaves only.

60 Guinea pig favourites include: apples, pears, cauliflower, sprouts, chicory and kale.

63 If you see your guinea pig eating his own droppings, do not think he has picked up a bad habit. It helps the guinea pig to obtain full goodness from his food.

61 You can feed plants from your garden, such as dandelion, groundsel, and chickweed. Marigold, nasturtiums, wallflowers, sweet peas and cornflowers also go down well.

66 Guinea pigs 'talk' to each other. They also use their voices when they are frightened, when they are warning other guinea pigs of danger, and when they are happy. As you get to know your pet, you will be able to understand what he is saying.

64 The best feeding plan is to provide two meals a day: the 'complete' diet plus hay in the morning, and fruit and vegetables with more hay in the evening.

67 Cooing is a sign that all is well; a mother guinea pig will often coo to her babies. If you have a very close relationship, your guinea pig may coo to you.

65 Hand-feeding will help your guinea pig to become more tame.

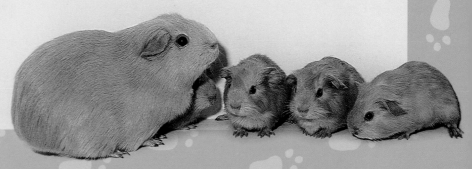

68 A high-pitched squeal is a warning that danger is close by. It is also a cry of pain or fear.

69 Chattering teeth means 'stay away', and it may be made to humans as well as to other guinea pigs. Watch out – this is one of the rare times when a guinea pig may bite.

70 When a guinea pig is really happy, he makes a gurgling sound. This could be at the sight of special food, the return of an old friend to the colony, or perhaps he is feeling especially pleased to see you!

71 Guinea pigs are active throughout the day – although they are at their liveliest in the evening.

22

75 If a guinea pig is approached by an enemy, he may 'play dead'— lying completely still on his back in an attempt to stop the attack. If you see your guinea pig doing this, it means he is very frightened.

72 Guinea pigs are able to see in colour.

73 Body language can give you clues as to how your guinea pig is feeling.

76 Friendly guinea pigs touch noses with each other – you will see members of the same group doing this.

74 A guinea pig that is lying fully stretched-out is relaxed and content.

23

77 A guinea pig looking for a fight (probably a sow) will stand up with her legs stiffened.

78 Jumping from a standing start is a special guinea pig habit. Why do they do it? Quite simply, they jump for joy.

79 A healthy guinea pig needs to live in a clean home. You will need to clean the hutch/cage every day, or every other day if your guinea pigs spend a lot of time in an exercise run.

80 Daily cleaning chores should involve removing droppings and wet bedding, cleaning food bowls, and checking the water-bottle. It is best to move your guinea pigs to the exercise run while you do this.

81 Once a week, all the bedding must be removed and replaced with fresh material.

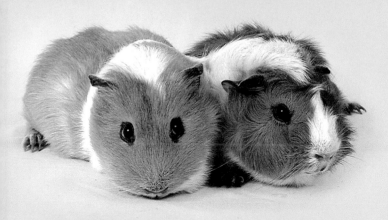

84 A weekly session will keep the smooth-haired varieties in good order. Rough-coated varieties (with whorls and rosettes) will need a daily brush.

82 Once a month, the hutch or cage should be thoroughly cleaned. Your pet store will sell a mild disinfectant that is safe for animals.

83 Your guinea pig will benefit from being groomed. You can start this as soon as he has settled in his new home.

85 The long-coated Peruvians (above) are strictly for the experts – their coat needs constant attention. The spectacular coat of a show guinea pig, which measures up to 20 inches (50 cms) in length, needs special care and protection.

86 Peruvians are born short-coated, with two rosettes on the rear. The hair grows upwards towards the ears, except for the hair behind the rosettes, which grows downwards.

87 Guinea pigs do not need to be bathed. The only times that your cavy may need cleaning is if he has been in a muddy enclosure, or his rear end has become soiled if he has been suffering from diarrhoea.

88 A guinea pig's teeth never stop growing. Sometimes they grow out of line, and do not wear down naturally. If your guinea pig drools or struggles to eat his food, his teeth may need clipping. Ask your vet to do this for you.

89 If you are going away on holiday, ask an experienced owner to call in morning and evening to look after your guinea pigs. Some pet stores offer a **boarding** service for small animals.

90 A guinea pig that is kept on soft bedding will need to have his nails clipped on a regular basis. Ask an experienced guinea pig keeper to help, or your vet will do the job for you.

91 The correct diet and housing should ensure your guinea pig stays fit and well. If he is unwell, he may show the followings signs:

- Runny eyes or nose
- Matted or soiled coat
- Difficulty eating
- Drooling saliva
- Heavy breathing
- Diarrhoea
- Loss of appetite
- Drinking more than usual.

92 Guinea pigs are very hard patients to treat, as many of the medicines that are safe to use on other small animals cannot be used on them.

93 Guinea pigs are ready to breed when they are just 12 weeks of age.

94 There are between two and four piglets in each litter.

95 The largest litter of guinea pigs recorded is 12 – born in a laboratory in 1972.

96 The piglets are born around 63 days after mating.

97 In the wild, guinea pigs are not born in burrows but on open ground. This means they have to be able to look after themselves right from the start.

98 For this reason, piglets are quite big when they are born, weighing about 3 oz (85 g).

99 They have a full coat, their eyes are open, and their teeth are already cut.

100 Within a few days of being born, piglets can begin to tackle solid food.

101 Guinea pigs are great fun to keep – watch out, or you will soon have a houseful!

GLOSSARY

Abyssinian: a guinea pig with a rough coat that is arranged in circular shapes.

Boar: a male guinea pig.

Boarding: a place where guinea pigs are looked after when their owners go on holiday.

Cavies: another name for guinea pigs.

Crossbred: a guinea pig whose parents are different breeds.

Hutch: outdoor housing.

Incas: an ancient people who lived in Peru, South America.

Long-haired: a guinea pig with a long coat, such as the Peruvian.

Marked: a guinea pig whose coat is a combination of colours.

Purebred: a guinea pig whose parents are the same breed.

Rex: a type of guinea pig that has a woolly coat.

Rodent: a type of gnawing animal that includes the rat, mouse and hamster.

Satin: a type of guinea pig that has a short, shiny coat.

Self: a guinea pig whose coat is one colour.

Smooth: a guinea pig with a short coat.

Sow: a female guinea pig.

MORE BOOKS TO READ

All About Your Guinea Pig
Bradley Viner
(Ringpress Books)

**Pet Owner's Guide to
the Guinea Pig**
Chris Henwood
(Ringpress Books)

Guinea Pigs (First Pet Series)
Kate Petty and George Thompson
(Barron's Juveniles)

**Guinea Pigs
(Nature Watch Series)**
Elvig Hansen
(Carolrhoda Books)

WEBSITES

Guinea pig favourites
www.pgaa.com/burrow/general/
guineapig.html

Cavy madness
www.cavymadness.com

Caring For Your Guinea Pig
www.petclubhouse.com/
guineapig/5033.htm

Cavies galore
www.caviesgalore.com

To find more websites about guinea pigs, use a good search engine to find one or more of these words: **cavies**, **guinea pigs**, **rodents**.

INDEX

Room for a Little One

Martin Waddell
Illustrated by Jason Cockcroft

ORCHARD BOOKS

It was a cold winter's night.
Kind Ox lay in his stable,
close to the side of the inn.

Old Dog came by.

He stopped, and looked into the stable.

"I need somewhere to rest," said Old Dog.

"Come inside," Kind Ox said.

"There's always room for a little one here."

Old Dog came in and lay down in the straw.

He nestled close to Kind Ox,

sharing the warmth of his stable.

Stray Cat peered in.

She saw Old Dog and she stopped.

Stray Cat arched her back and her fur bristled.

"I'll not chase you," said Old Dog.

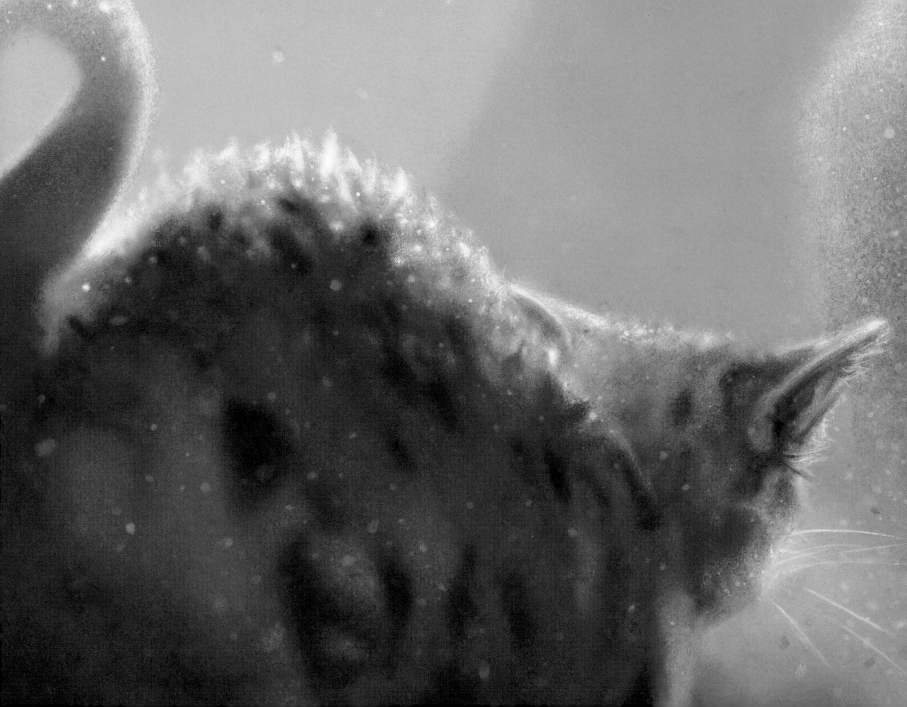

"Come inside," Kind Ox said.

"There's always room for a little one here."

Stray Cat came into the stable.
She curled up in the straw,
close to the friends she had found,
purring and twitching her tail.

Small Mouse stopped at the door of the stable.

She saw Stray Cat and she quivered with fear.

"You're safe here, I won't harm you," said Stray Cat.

"Come inside," Kind Ox said.

"There's always room for a little one here."

Small Mouse scurried in.

She nestled down warm in the straw,

in the peace of the stable.

Then Tired Donkey came.

Joseph led him along.

Mary rode on Tired Donkey's back.

Joseph was cold and Mary was weary,

but there was no room at the inn.

"Where will my baby be born?" Mary asked.

"Come inside," Kind Ox called to Tired Donkey.

"There's always room for a little one here."

Tired Donkey brought Mary into the stable.
Joseph made her a warm bed in the straw,
to save her from the cold of the night.

And so Jesus was born with the animals around Him;
Kind Ox, Old Dog, Stray Cat, Small Mouse, and
Tired Donkey all welcomed Him to the
warmth of their stable.

That cold winter's night,
beneath the star's light …

…a Little One came for the world.